A Breath Of Fresh Air

poetry Pt today

A Breath Of Fresh Air

Edited by
Rebecca Mee

First published in Great Britain in 1998 by Poetry
Today, an imprint of
Penhaligon Page Ltd, 12 Godric Square, Maxwell Road,
Peterborough. PE2 7JJ

A Catalogue record for this book is available from the
British Library

ISBN 1 86226 520 8

Typesetting and layout, Penhaligon Page Ltd, England.
Printed and bound by Forward Press Ltd, England

Foreword

A Breath Of Fresh Air is a compilation of poetry, featuring some of our finest poets. The book gives an insight into the essence of modern living and deals with the reality of life today. We think we have created an anthology with a universal appeal.

There are many technical aspects to the writing of poetry and *A Breath Of Fresh Air* contains free verse and examples of more structured work from a wealth of talented poets.

Poetry is a coat of many colours. Today's poets write in a limitless array of styles: traditional rhyming poetry is as alive and kicking today as modern free-verse. Language ranges from easily accessible to intricate and elusive.

Poems have a lot to offer in our fast-paced 'instant' world. Reading poems gives us an opportunity to sit back and explore ourselves and the world around us.

Contents

He Gave His All

There was a boy born long ago
Who loved Jesus so
He followed the crowd to wherever it may be
For the saviour he wanted to see
The crowd was so large and he was so small
He didn't think he would see Jesus at all.

But that was not so he had to play a part
For Jesus knew he was there right from the start
With five small loaves and two small fishes
Jesus granted the little boys wishes
Jesus blessed and broke the bread
Then the great multitude were fed.

Five thousand gathered there that day
To hear what Jesus had to say
Then a miracle took place that they were all fed
With two small fishes and five small loaves of bread
Thanks to the little boy who gave his all
When he heard the saviour call.

H M Regan

Candle Power

Peering curiously into crevices
Of the past, the man prowls around
                    the church's
decrepit age of loneliness
Trying to see what he can sniff
Out in the enveloping darkness,
Or nostalgically, hoping to catch a whiff
Of the incense of England's lost holiness.

Walking back along a briary path
Into an age of innocence,
He finds himself at the edge of a cliff,
For here the road of the senses
Like the route of common-sense
Stops short: rather, here we all fall short
And hang questioningly in mid-air.
How do we go from here? Where?

Can stone speak to stone?
Can words linger in a church's ruin,
            even metaphorically?
Ornate stone being but the outdoor wear
Of the church corporate, one bone
Of a saint could surely tell more,
A bone that once was cousin to a heart,
A heart that solved the mystery
Of its own mystical identity.
Could Faith be removed surgically?
The sun may shine on high windows,
But only heart can speak to heart.

Mary Frances Mooney

Golden Jubilee

When first I called you to my Vineward years ago
>
> my life to share,

My yoke was sweet, my burden light, my noble cross
>
> easy to bear.

And later when the work was hard and labourers few
>
> you faltered not,

But welcomed joyfully my father's will in all
>
> and shared my lot.

And when o'er sinners hardened hearts the evil one seemed
>
> to sway,

Your countless 'Ave's' and my mothers prayers have fought
>
> and won the day.

How many knew but little of my love until your prayer
>
> had pierced the skies,

In pleading that my precious blood
>
> their souls might spare.

Into the past has rolled those fifty years of labour
>
> and all for me-

While I have counted every step that you have taken
>
> hence, this great Jubilee-

And as a reward for this long life of sacrifice
                                        you shall have part
In my eternal joy, and find your name in 'Gold'
                                        upon my heart.

M McCartan

Piece Of Heaven

My piece of Heaven
Shines in glistening array
White Lilies are strewn
To make a path to show
And guide the way.
White gowns are laid in numerical line
Halos beaming light, awakes
The stranger from his sleep
Come, wine, dine,
Join the Saints, Angel Gabriel
Has found a piece of Heaven
Cherubs playing harps so gay
Float on that cloud and dream away.

D Thomson

Shepherdesses (On The Ordination Of Women To The Priesthood)

Once there were shepherds who tended their flocks
And led them to pastures away from the rocks;
Fed their minds daily with words full of hope,
Were there is their troubles, and helped them to cope;
Guided their eyes ever upwards to God,
Directed their feet on the roads saints had trod;
Went out and preached to the world in their search
To bring all to faith and to life in the Church;
Baptised the children, and adults who came
To give their allegiance to Christ's holy name;
Nourished their souls with the body and blood
Of Christ their redeemer, whose love like a flood
Pours down on his people, wherever they are,
And draws them towards him from near and from far;
Heard their confessions, and gave them God's love,
Dispensing the power they received from above;
Gave them God's blessing, to brighten their hearts
With all of the joy and the hope that imparts;
Prayed for their needs, like a mother would do,
And watched as their faith and their holiness grew;
Held up a vision of life without end,
With God in his heaven, with Christ as a friend;
Encouraged the doubting, and tried of their best
To comfort the poor and the weak and distressed;
Strengthened their minds with the Gospel of Christ,
And hoped that they'd not by the world be enticed;

Once only shepherds were charged with these roles,
But now shepherdesses can care for our souls.

Eileen Morrison

Crucified Devotion

Regard me forth
We are the same
As in your naked thoughts I'm slain
My sacrificial life bears true
The deepest thoughts revealed in you
Do you seek peace?
Does your life force grow
In harmony with the world you know?
Will you seek to share your richest vein
Pursued down to the final grain?
In sacrifice each nail drives through
Upon the cross may God bless you

Shaun Murray

I'm Set Free

My Lord, you have turned my heart around,
And placed me on solid ground,
Where once my feet slipped and slide,
Now I stand firmly by your side,
My eyes were closed at first,
I couldn't see this new birth,
But Born Again I have become,
Washed and cleansed by God's only son,
Holy Spirit has revived my life,
Thrown out all the strife,
My eyes are open,
Now I see,
Through Christ Jesus - I'm set free!

Paula Aitken

Father God

We must always listen to you Father God
Even when we believe we have learnt all there is to know.
Evil thoughts abound within us that flow
Rapidly and exhaust us Father God

Take us in hand with instant kindness Father God
Fashion us into your loving ways
Constantly speak to us in your still small voice
Make us listen to you Father God.

You sent your wonderful son Jesus Christ Father God
To bring us to heel and share his miraculous life
Though he was cruxified by non understanding people
He did leave his disciples to continue his work Father God.

You and Jesus Christ are more than man's best friends, Father
God
Much love and kindness has been given to those in need
Especially the blind and those with horrific diseases
People, thank you so much Father God.

Listening to you when reading your Holy Bible, Father God
We see the goodness over flowing
What a wonderful example you have created knowing
One day we will dispatch our hearts to you Father God.

Readiness to love you Father God
Must take priority, giving us
The opportunity to prepare for your son's coming without fuss,
May the waiting be over soon, thank you, Father God.

Alma Montgomery Frank

I Give My Life

I have promised to my Lord,
To follow in his ways,
I know he's there to help me,
Throughout the coming days.

I praise your Holy name O God,
My love for you I give
Show me how to be like you,
The way I ought to live.

Make me true and righteous
Help me to be humble
When things go wrong, or I stray
Teach me not to grumble

Help me to live my life for you,
In all things great and small,
Be there to help me always,
When I'm weak and fall.

I worship and adore you.
Your love for me is known
Teach me to praise and love you,
In me these things are sown.

Show me the path to follow,
As I take my daily walk
O God, I need your guidance
And love to hear you talk

Be with me in the things I do
That I may do them right
Help me, be with me in my day,
Give peace to rest at night.

I give my life to Jesus,
Only Lord, let it be,
Filled with love and praises,
Consecrated Lord to thee.

Bernard Jones-Baynam

I Need A Helping Hand

We live our lives the best
We can but now I need a
Helping hand a gentle whisper
A silent pray just to say
Someone cares as all the
Tears are hard to hide so
Please my Lord come by my
Side. Will walk together hand
In hand for only you can
Understand.

Mick Young

The Way And The Light

I am the Way that leads to my Father
And the Light that shows you the path

So hear me one and all,
From kings and shepherds, and an oxen stall
From days in the desert tempted,
To days of water and wine
Days of loaves and fishes
Days of sacramental dishes
Times of betrayal through love
Or betrayal through spite
Still and all two things remain
I am the Way and I am the Light

Philip Tyler

Day Of Joy

There is a day, of joy
      That will come
For every mother, father,
      Daughter and son

Heavenly music will make
      The sound,
Happy people dancing around,
      Love flows from the sky,
Will reflect in your eye.

On the day of joy,
      Day of joy.

John Booth

A Listening Ear

God's our heavenly Father,
He's in every breath of air
He taught us how to reap and sow
He taught us how to care
He taught us good from evil
And showed us how to pray
He is always there when needed
To help us on our way.
He's brought a special meaning
Into this world of ours
He gave us trees and forests,
Butterflies and flowers
He's never too busy to listen
To what we have to say
Because we are all his children
He's there for us come what may
So when our burden's too heavy
And we need to lighten our load,
Just pray to God our Father
And he'll help us along the road.

Theresa Fitzgerald

Cold Falls The Rain -

Cold falls the rain in November,
Cold falls the rain
On the headstones in the little churchyard,
Where they sleep, who will rise again.

Sleep well, beloved!
Though death has torn us apart,
And though Time and Space divide us,
Your love lives warm in my heart.

Cold is the rain in November,
Cold is the rain,
But safe in the earth are the blossoms
That spring will bring forth again.

Sleep well, beloved!
Safely at rest in the earth
Are those who will come like the flowers,
At the heavenly spring's rebirth.

M H Seymour

My Prayer

Make me
An instrument
Of Your praise
A symphony played
In the lives of others
Make my life a manuscript
For others to hold and read
Allow them to receive pleasure
From what they see and hear
Give my heart the joy of praise
Let my words be serene and sweet
And my being a melody that is contagious
Flowing like drifting strains over barren deserts
Let my heart be at peace to hear the strumming of Your words
Keep me in harmony and allow me to dance with the Holy Spirit
So that I can constantly minister to souls out of tune with Thee

P J Byers

An Easter Poem

It was upon a Friday, why do we call it good
When Jesus Christ our Saviour hung on a cross of wood
He had no right to be there he had done nothing wrong
But chose to take the punishment which should to us belong.
He thought that you had left him Dear Father up above
But really in his inmost heart he knew that you were love
We should have born the suffering for selfishness and sin
Not just stand by and watch and leave it all to him
But on the Sunday morning you rose up from the grave
We saw how much you really cared for those you came to save
Yet still we disobey you and do not do your will
But when we look upon that cross we know you love us still

W G H Tickner

Untitled

Christmas never did mean much to me, the point of it I could not
see.
Eating drinking bored to tears, been going on for donkeys years.
Relatives round you can't stand, pretending to be happy shaking
hands.
Useless Christmas presents you don't need, millions starving they
have no feed.
Forget about them there out of sight, just make merry through the
night.
Why do we do it year by year, don't ask me pal here have some beer.
But wasn't Jesus Christ born today, perhaps he was but who can say.
If we don't believe why do we say, have a Happy Christmas Day.
It's just tradition it makes no sense, if you happen to be sitting on the
fence.
I've never given it much thought, religion something I've never
sought.
Who knows if Jesus was even real, I've heard it's just something that
you feel.
There again old Tom did change, his love for booze it simply waned.
He don't swear now except when mad, he used to be a real Jack the
lad.
Now he says Jesus really lives, love N peace is what he gives.
I've seen such a change in him, now he says he can't stand sin.
I'm not too bad well it don't show, I'll go to heaven that I know.
Everyone goes to the same place, hole in the ground or the other
place.
But what about the real inner me, that bit even the surgeons can not
see.
That part Tom said would never die, he's my mate but would he lie.
He said I've got a space within, made for God yet filled with sin.
Perhaps there's something to this Jesus guy, if he died for me I
wonder why.
I really wish I could believe, then perhaps I too could receive.
The holy spirit Tom told me about. I know deep down I'd like to
shout.
Jesus is real at last I know, he is alive he told me so.

I can not believe it is no use, guess I'll go on tightening the noose.
Till the grim reaper calls my name, heaven or hell it's just the same.
Then at least I'll know for sure, if Jesus ever knocked at my door.
I'll tell him then why I didn't believe, if given the chance I will
                                                            receive.
The Lord Jesus Christ as my saviour too, but will he say it's now too
                                                    late for you
You lived your life you made your choice, you would not listen to
                                            my voice.
But I never heard you speak, never, but then did you seek.
Were you never told about my life, how I came to earth as a
                                                    sacrifice.
How I died to take your sin away, so you could dwell with me one
                                                            day.

Don Goodwin

Who Is Jesus?

Jesus is a friend of mine
A special one you know,
He came to earth to die for me
That the world His love might show.
But while upon this earth He walked,
The road was long and bare,
For all the people that passed Him by
Would stop, but didn't really care.
You see - He came to earth for a reason
To do His Fathers will,
The people that knew Him long ago
Would His Fathers plan fulfil.
For when they had to make a choice
A murderer they preferred,
But Jesus in His Holiness never uttered a word.
They whipped and beat Him till He bled,
How cruel and wicked they were,
They hung Him high on a wooden cross
And a cry of forgiveness was heard.
But three days later Jesus returned
To His family and Friends,
For Jesus overcame His death
And death, for us, has no end.
And we today can still hurt Him bad
By rejecting His undying love,
He wants to become, a very special friend
But a willing heart, you must have.
He is so precious, so very real, He's with me all the time
I thank Him so much for dying for me.
And I'm so glad that Jesus is mine!

Jacqueline Ware

A Prayer To Our Father

Whenever we feel low
And don't know what to do
Just kneel and say a prayer
And God will answer you
He gives you peace of mind
And lets you choose your way
But he's never far from you
Each and every day
For his son Jesus, was crucified
He died to save us all
And now he's seated by his father
And he listens to our call
For God never turns away from us
He listens and knows our ways
So whenever we have done wrong
He listens to us pray
It's then we need to say I've sinned
And tell him all we've done
He gives us then our penance
But we are still his chosen ones.

Sally Elizabeth Burton

The Divine Plan

One Friday morn soon after dawn
They hung upon a tree
The only Son of God Himself,
Who died to set us free.

When evening came they buried Him,
The One Who'd come to save.
Nicodemus bought the spices,
And Joseph gave the grave.

The third day brought the women
Their last respects to pay
To be greeted by an angel
Who'd rolled the stone away.

The sepulchre was empty now,
The grave clothes still unrolled.
'He is risen,' cried the angel,
'The others must be told.'

Quite soon as every Christian knows
They met their Lord again
When Jesus taught that Heaven's joys
Will follow death and pain.

For forty days he stayed with them
And spoke of love and light;
Then to his throne above He went,
Ascending in their sight.

He told the angels all he'd done
Whilst on His earthly stay
And how He hoped the world would walk
Along His chosen way.

Said He, 'Twelve men I've set aside
And each of them I've taught
To spread My word where'er he goes
Lest it should come to nought.'

'For strength and help in this great work
They all depend on Me,
But I Myself depend on them
As you must surely see.'

'Suppose they fail,' the angels said,
'For weak we know is Man!'
'I pray they won't,' the Lord replied,
'I have no other plan.'

C Champneys Burnham

Simon Peter Remembers

I remember well the incident, we were busy with the net,
Fishing in Lake Galilee long e'er the sun was set,
Then, looking on the lakeside a Man we saw ahead;
'Come with Me and fishers be, of men' was what He said.
I cannot say why right away we took Him at His word
But could it be that we could see that this was Christ the Lord?
One day when we were washing nests close by Gennesaret's shore;
He told us to fish deeper and we would then catch more.
With little hope and much less faith, the Master we obeyed,
And lo, our nets with fish were filled which in two boats were laid.
'Twas then I saw His power supreme; I fell upon my knees
'Lord Jesus, I'm a simple man; leave me,' was my plea.
James and John were frightened too - but Jesus said to me;
'From now you will be catching men; let all your fears flee.'
I think that this was when we knew that Jesus was the Lord,
The true Messiah whom we sought - we learned to trust His word.
I'm such a sinner, yet He said my name would Cephas be;
A rock on which He'd build His church for all the world to see.
We ate and slept and worked with Him, His miracles we shared;
We saw His love for all mankind; we knew how much He cared.
And yet - and yet I failed my Lord in hour of greatest need;
When challenged I denied my God, His words I did not heed,
'Before the cock crows twice,' He said, 'My Name you will deny
Not once, not twice but thrice,' He said; 'Not true Lord!' was my cry.
Jesus then was crucified and we were so afraid;
Behind locked doors we hid ourselves; we dare not speak His Name.
But in that room, though doors were closed, Lord Jesus stood within;
'Peace to you, go forth with power; forgive the peoples' sin'.
Our Lord had died, but rose again; great joy filled every heart.
For now we knew He'd conquered death, from Him we would never
                                                            part.

Nora Marsh

Christ Is Risen

I wish I had been there that Easter morning,
Among the women visiting his tomb.
How tearfully they must have talked,
Their hearts so full of gloom
I wonder who was first to notice
The great stone had been rolled away,
Then see the two men dressed in white,
And hear the angels say,
'He is not here, He's risen!'

O, with what wonder they would hurry
This news to all his friends to tell,
Scarcely believing it could really happen,
Yet their gloom was starting to dispel.
And as he came to them on the Emmaus Road,
And in the upper room and by the sea,
They knew with certainty a miracle had happened
That tho' they'd seen him die on Calvary,
Now he lived again.

And still he lives, He is alive forever,
Yes, He's alive, empowered now to save,
And in his hands he holds the keys
Of death, hell and the grave.
And unto those who own his name
He grants the faith to know
Tho' it defies all human reason
It is gloriously, wonderfully so.
The tomb is empty - Christ is risen!

Anne Workman

An Easter Prayer

The glory and the beauty of Easter passes by,
Once more I am reminded of your Son who came to die.
He came to die for me Lord, for sinful wicked me,
It makes me feel so humble - He could have left me be!
But He is love incarnate and He came to set me free
From self and hate and fear and death to glorious victory.
How can I ever thank Him? How can I ever show
How very much I owe Him who sets my heart aglow?
Oh help me Lord to follow in the steps that you have trod
The steps that lead to heaven and to our Father God.

Eira Smith

Easter Morn

The flower were there to greet Him
On that first Easter morn.
When Jesus from the grave arose,
And new life to earth was born.
The birds they sang in chorus,
A welcome for to bring
And Angels in the Heavens,
Sang glory to their King.

Jesus rose triumphant
That morning from the grave.
Knowing if they believed in Him
The whole world He would save.
He broke the power of evil,
He conquered death and sin,
Bringing here on earth to man
A tranquil peace within

Let us rejoice with Jesus,
Sing our love and praise
With bright and happy chorus
Loud our anthems raise.
Giving to God the glory
For His sacrifice,
Of His own beloved Son
Our Saviour Jesus Christ

E Pate

Easter Promise

As one turns to the rugged cross
One contemplates heavens precious things
Of time tinged cantilles of hope
As Jesus rose from the dead
So mankind could lay in a gentler bed
On reminisces of the betrayal by man
Of God since time began
As Mary weeps for the lost souls
Many men come to rest in ghoul's
For it is a forgiving God
Who knows no boundaries of love
Who resides in the place above
And as the clock strikes midday in country fields
A prayer for many bare souls reveal
But as the birds fly away on a winters morn
Debating why God's son was so dejected and forlorn
As spring comes around
Most repent to God's love abound

Finnan Boyle

A Vigil Prayer

Oh Lord, as I kneel here and pray
To You, dear Lord, this Good Friday,
As on this day you had to die
All my prayers have You in mind.

Oh Lord, How can my prayers begin
While in this world there's so much sin.
We forget the pain you had that day;
For all lost souls to You I pray.

Oh Lord while on that cross in pain
You promised to come to earth again,
To save our world and give us faith
And remember your life and your fate.

Oh Lord, while here in church I kneel,
Here in my heart your presence feel,
I feel dear Lord you are present;
To be here with you is so pleasant.

Oh Lord, my heart is full of pain
For what we did to You that day.
I hope dear Lord that when I die
A place in Heaven for me you'll find.

Francis Allen

Easter Celebration

Spring brings us all the chance of re-birth
as we celebrate 'Oestre' and Christ's rising again
up from earth.
We recall the days of torment and gloom,
but Christ thro' his resurrection says 'I am just
in another room.'
Christ tells us He is with us, each one
who trusts and believes the message of His love,
for He lives on.

Oestre, or Easter, has a message for all,
it shows how new life springs up with fresh chance
overcoming downfall.
Jesus the Messiah came, He died for all our sins,
He rose again to prove that death, and evil's ways,
no longer wins.
Easter, happy Eastertime, is here to greet
the world, and free it from its woes and vice -
if Christ we meet.

Spring brings us all the chance to renew
our faith in Christ, now Easter's here for all again,
for me and you.
We celebrate Oestre, Christ's message of love
to share the renewal of life which is given freely
by God above.
Rejoice in the Saviour, Rejoice in the Lord!
Easter is here, the promise is kept, for Jesus
is the Risen Word.

Ann Voaden

My Prayer This Easter
For Strength

Arise and awaken oh my soul and be glad
For the wonderful Easter day I have had.
Give thanks for the dawn of this new day.
In which to love, to laugh, to work and to play.
As the sun rises high to shed its light,
Make this Easterday to be kind and do right.
Let the love of God that is in my heart,
Pour forth on all of whom I am a part,
So . . . when the sun sets in the golden west,
I can thank God this Easterday, I did my very best.

William Price

Bedtime Worry

Where you ever frightened of the dark, Grandma,
And lightning and thunder?
Did the shadows in your room jump out,
And the bed have creatures under?

Did you listen to funny noises Granddad,
Real scary in the night.
When your Mum and Dad, had gone to bed,
And there wasn't any light?

Will you hold my hand tonight Grandma,
While Granddad looks around,
And can I stay downstairs tonight,
Until the monster's found?

I *know* there are no monsters,
It's really all pretend,
But just stay by my side tonight,
And I'll *always* be your friend.

Gwyneth Cleworth

Summer Morning On Malvern

The sun is far risen now, a jewel in the sky,
And Malvern lies prone, silhouetted and high;
Reducing long shadows, and firing my dreams,
As I climb up these hills now, on cold granite seams.

Past spring water's bubbling, and the spurt of a well,
Above Great Malvern's Priory, with its far-chiming bell,
To this place of day trippers, and hikers and me,
Where there's echoes of cavemen, and earthworks to see.

Forget-me-nots and foxgloves glow damp with the dew,
As I walk on cropped grass to the beacon's high view;
Resplendent the horizon in this haze of far heat,
As a cricket jumps past me, and I rest on a seat.

And a lazy noon sun heats the shimmering green
Of a long line of peaks, far off like a dream;
As now a long adder slinks slowly by me,
Alive, low and needling; in the sun so free.

Ed Tudor

Christmas Is Coming

Christmas is coming, I've made out my list,
I want to make sure that nothing is missed.

The children want toys, and games, and things,
The older nieces want diamond earrings!
Two tins of biscuits, a bottle of wine,
Chocolates for Auntie - that'll do fine.
A razor for Dad, a kettle for Mom,
I'm not really sure where the money'll come from!
And what can I get for old Uncle Fred?
I'm sure he wants something - what was it he said?

And then there's the cards - I've sent eighty three,
I hope all of them will send one to me.
If not, then next year, they'll not get another
I'm not sending cards to those that don't bother!

Then there's the food - so much to prepare,
So that we can all have a true 'Christmas Fare'.
There's turkey to cook, and mince pies to bake,
And I haven't got round to icing the cake!

Then there's the tree to buy and to dress,
I go for plastic - it's not such a mess!
There's streamers to hang from highest of heights,
And if they will work, there's Christmas tree lights!

Now that I'm ready, nothing is missing,
I've even got mistletoe ready for kissing!

What a performance, I often think 'why?'
But listen - was that a babe I heard cry?

David Morgan

Childhood Memories (1940's)

I sit quietly in the chair and let my mind slip back
To when I was a child sat on my granny's lap
Her large soft bosom on which to lay my head
'That's enough now, I've work to do', the words I would dread.
Summer in the garden, snapdragons on my fingertips
Teatime, bread and margarine tasty to my lips.
Cold winter days, clothes horse round the open fire
Lodgers moving in and out, another room for hire
Granny working endlessly giving them some rest
Making me clothes from coupon gifts, wanting to do her best
Happy hours of playing in mother's high-heeled shoes
Or with my dolls, with few from which to choose
Snuggling up at bedtime as granny tucked me in
Trying to stay awake, knowing I couldn't win.
Christmas paper chains, handmade with paste and hung above
The joy of stockings filled with little but filled with love
Puddings stirred with eagerness, coins and wishes added too
Turkey plucked and stuffed, mince pies as well - just a few.
Long hot summers, odd days on the beach
Any more than that completely beyond our reach
Happy, happy school days, keenness to learn
Children's wet shoes around a fire that wouldn't burn.
Bottles of milk at play time, drunk through a straw
Lots of games to play, skipping, hopscotch and ball
A dose of syrup of figs at the end of every week
Goose grease on our chest for colds, kept us in the peak
Many, many years have passed away since all of this
But memories remain of which, to enter is bliss.

Veronica Quainton

Solitude

The air is still
And yet I know not why the bluebells and the daffodils
Are waving on the hill:
Against the sky they prance and sway
For light and joy has shone this day;
And so they dance
Like fronds with dagger leaf, green of the first fresh buds of Spring:
And o'er the heath
The lark begins to sing a plaintiff air,
A constant cry - hovering above
And here I feel that God is nigh.

The silence of the misty hills
So gently falls and now my heart it softly stills
And all my mind is peace and calm:
And beauty calls, for wondrous is this nature's balm.
The twilight comes, the earth is still
And midnight stars bedeck the night,
And creeping creatures move no more -
The bats begin their swooping flight
Out for the kill.

This transient time
Beguiles my heart and soothes and calms my troubled thoughts
The sadness that surrounds our clime
Methinks myself - 'twas all for nought.
For here is peace -
And here is joy, 'tis nature that can tell us true
There is a God, there is a love
For child and girl, for man and boy;
It is for me, it is for you.

Mollie D Earl

Untitled

The sun is streaming through my window
Heralding the start of another day
A loud dawn chorus makes me open my eyes
Cheering me as I lay.
My breathing is not too laboured.
Will this be a good day?
Shall I be able to get out of bed
Washed and dressed
And stay that way?

It's worth a go
But I don't know.
The effort seems too much.
And yet I must
I cannot be beaten.
This thing is not going to drag me down.
It cannot win.

Think of the sound of the birds
And the welcoming sun.
The flowers are blooming.
Forget my cough and shortness of breath.
Just rest after washing
'Til things settle down.
Enjoy the day
Think of good things
Not bad.

Maureen Godwin

Memories

I often think of some-one I knew a while ago
Who used to live quite near to me - the second in a row
Of terraced houses behind my cottage by the sea
We grew quite close to one another as close as close could be!

She was always very busy - had so much to do
Caring for all the family - her youngest not yet two
Helping with her husband's work as he was self employed
Always bright and cheery doing work which she enjoyed.

I often had her children for just an hour of two
They used to love to come across - they called me Auntie Sue
I often took them for a walk - I enjoyed this so much
As I was a wee bit lonely and liked to keep in touch.

Then suddenly I had to leave my cottage on the hill
And make my way to Scotland - my Mum was taken ill
And I was there for several months just sitting by her side
And did not come back home until after she had died.

I returned to Cornwall on a wet, autumnal day
And it was quite late evening when I saw that something lay
On the doormat - just a scribbled note- it was from my friend
Full of grateful thanks from the beginning to the end.

It was only in the postscript that things became more clear
As to why they'd had to leave the home she had held so dear
'The work has not gone well of late' and then I felt her pain
As I read in smaller writing 'Joe's hit the bottle again'.

Greta E Bray

My Love And I

As we were walking out one day,
My friend and I along the way.
'twas on a sunny afternoon,
Somewhere around the midst of June,
We met two boys, one we knew not,
The other we did, quite a lot.
He introduced us to his friend,
Cupid an arrow to my heart did send.
I fell in love upon that day,
And he did too, I'm pleased to say.
We wed and raised a family,
Two girls, two boys, my love and me.
The years passed our love grew and grew,
Oh yes we had a row or two.
We struggled oft' financially
But were rich in love as we could be.
Grandchildren were born as time went by,
And how the years seemed to fly.
We thought together we'd always be,
Living our lives quite happily.
It broke my heart upon that day,
God gently took my love away.
But I know that someday he will be,
Waiting there in heaven for me.

Maureen Wilkinson

The Tragedy

The tragedy happened on a Friday night,
A boat sailed out in the dusky light.
Only half an hour in sail
When the boat lurched over yet there was no gale.

The sea flat calm that cold winter's night
Visibility good was the seaman's sight.
Passengers around the decks, inside and out,
Well wrapped up in their woollies, no doubt!

Oh what a night! It started so well.
Excitement abound like a musical bell.
Then when it happened, it happened so quick
Flat on their sides in water so thick.

Personal belongings and the tables contents
Flew around the rooms, in an awful stew.
The people were flung this way and that.
The ship settled down on its side lying flat.

The water poured in with a waterfall's strength.
The cold and the numbness the passengers felt.
The panic and the fear as the lights all went out,
And with darkness surrounding, the people in doubt.

Would they ever escape from this watery tomb?
Have faith, trust in God, were their prayers so sincere.
The rescue teams came at a speed so quick
To do what they could at that scene so sick.

Heroic activities for all to see,
The helping and caring without a fee.
A man swimming by, a babe in his teeth,
The human made bridges so more could get free.

Comforting the young child who thought she would die
A very young women felt strength from her sigh.
The child says 'A good girl she's been all her life.'
'And never told lies!' What a terrible night.

Pauline Stewart

The Food Fair

Yesterday we went to the fair
It made me stand and stare.
This wasn't any old kind,
Not the sort that you'll find.
But it was brill as you'll see
And there I had my tea.
This is called the Food Fair,
It made me stare.
The food was lovely
The drinks were bubbly,
(this is what there was) . . .
For main there was,
Veg, chicken bolognese and pork chops,
Pizza, chips, cheese and hot dogs
The desert was a dream
With Ginger men, lollipops and ice-cream
And three things which I thought were fake
Buns, pie and chocolate cake.
And also there was fruit
Apples, berries and grapefruit.
Fizzy drinks, milk and juice for you,
With tea, coffee and beer too.
Why don't you come next time?
I'm sure that you'll think it's fine.

Clare Mills (13)

A Ball At The Great Hall

A multitude of candles lights the great hall
The orchestra strikes up as a waltz is called
Rustling petticoats swing across the floor
As ladies are embraced and guided all before

As gentlemen convey a greeting as they meet
Their roving eyes beckon to each girl that's sweet
But chaperons too must be plied with compliments
If their young charge is allowed just one more dance

Punch and champagne the drink of the day
And as genteel lips sip, courtship is paid
The music then strikes up a welcoming note
As once again partners hold each other close

At the end of the ball young hearts beat fast
Has their new found love, come to last
A kiss on a gloved hand eyes now filled with tears
A time of their lives they will recall so clear

The music now has faded, guests depart into the night
Each carriage awaits, then gently fades from sight
Some hearts are broken others now stand tall
As the great doors shut, and a stillness covers all.

Gillian Mullett

Here And Now

It is now -
It will never be this now again.
Similar maybe, but never the same.
Another now comes, then still another
But - never this now again.

It is here -
Never again the same here as now
Always and everywhere changes somehow.
Harvest today followed spring's sowing.
Today's here and now is already fast going.

It is us -
Just us together, one with the other
Away from all kin, even brother and mother.
Grandparents die, children are born,
Night follows noon, noon follows morn.

It is choice -
What we do now is all we can choose
Acceptance is gain, to fight is to lose.
Today it is 'us', our 'now', our 'here' -
A beautiful cameo, precious and dear.

Grace Blackie

New White Trainers

Like new white trainers with unworn tread
Innocence in the school yard has no street cred
It has to be tainted
           Lived in
     Scuffed
           Used
     Abused
Before its intrinsic value is recognised

By such time as its credible
The stains are indelible
No amount of washing
          Smiling
     Polishing
            Giggling
    Re-sole-ing
            Re-soul-ing
    Resolving
           Dissolving
    Disowning
Will return the whiter than white
Innocent bliss
       Of the 10-year-old in M&S jeans
Who wonders what 'double entendre' means
              And feels confused
By the strange-shaped ladies on page three of the news
And knows the rejection of having too much shine
             On your shoes

Steve Lawson

No Time

Rushing here, rushing there -
never a moment to whisper a prayer.
Never to ask Him to guide our way,
or to seek help, to plan our day -
To ask forgiveness and say we're sorry,
always we're in too great a hurry.
But still He waits for us - unseen
'till we turn back and upon Him lean,
He is always there, with welcoming arms,
where we may find His blessed calm.

Iris Lloyd

The Planter Of The Bomb

That devastating sound, the blast that maims and kills
does not feel itself the pain it yields.
'Tis people made of flesh and blood who would describe their
feelings strong, should they, could they but some have gone.
It may not be their will to plant the bomb or destroy for sake
of such but principles of worth no longer stand where purposed
of ill be carried out.
Who really suffers the Pain?
Not the dead. It's all over for them.
'Tis their loved ones left behind to cope as best they can.
The injured ones who have to learn to live with defected limbs,
to shock, to situations which remind them of
That Bomb Blast Day.
Ah, but what of they who placed it there.
Long after purposed have gone and praise for services rendered
are erased and forgotten, they are the ones who suffer the pain
not only their foes.
When every successive bomb proclaims again the devastation of
that day, recalling vividly and with clarity to their minds.
For a fleeting moment the secret thoughts of the planter have
caught one unaware.
Was it I who blew those innocent people into eternity, not
allowing them the privileges I enjoy, my wife my family, indeed
my life and health.
Oh, how I wanted to defuse that bomb but counted the consequences
too great.
It took no boldness to plant it there any stupid person can do
what they are told they must.
If only I had had the courage to obey the conscience deep within.
Now too late to disconnect, the blast has gone.
Only time is left to reflect and recall the destruction done
by the Planter of the Bomb.

David Brunskill

48

Holidays

A time for refreshment
Leaving work behind us
Time for reflection
Gone from what duty binds us

Relaxing on a sun drenched beach
Or walking in the rain
Exploring by cycle or car
The many places near or far

Near rivers or by mountains tall
Grandeur there for one and all
A picnic near some wandering sheep
A quiet place to have a sleep

A friendly face which has a smile
A cosy chat to last a while
A lovely meal to stop your hunger
A feeling that you're now much younger

A time to say, dear I love you
The worries can rise above you
Are gone forever in the night
This rest has made all things right

Primrose Harvey

Time

The people of this day and age have no time
to stop and stare.
At the wonders of Nature's fair.
Their little lives are full of worry
because they always have to hurry.
Sometimes one may ask of me
why can't I stop and stare with thee.
And I answer with a smile
may be you can after the next weary mile.

They know nothing of Nature's changing face
as they hurry to and fro, at such a pace.
They say that I am lucky to stop and look
they make one feel just like a crook.
What they don't understand is that
I am destined to travel those weary miles
for as long as time continues to pile

You see I stopped and stared to long
now I can never hurry and be gone.

C Ash

Lady Julian Of Norwich

Straight from the heart of the King of Kings
The message from Lady Julian rings,
Down the passage of all the years.
To calm our woes and heal our fears
All Shall Be Well.

Through the deepest depths of the blackest night
To the upward heights of thy wondrous light,
Rings loud and clear, rings deep and low.
Through grace upon grace to help us know
All Shall Be Well.

Joyce Townsend

Precious Moments
Musings and Memories

'Life's just the strangest mixture
of happy and sad things -
almost like a pot-pourri
of colours, scents, that brings
to memory a kaleidoscope
of days and times, on wings
long past.
Forgotten hours of joy;
again, the offerings
of Former Times -
The petals stirred,
releasing fragrances
that springs
to fill the heart and mind -
Before the spirit onward wings.

Joan Peggy Croft

People

(Thos poem was written in a relaxed mood taking a quick glance at groups of people in the world today.)

Some people are happy all day -
travelling along in a pilgrim way.
Others dig their toes in the sand -
hoping to make this a permanent land.
Some people, worship God on their knees -
following the call as they see it to be.
Others strive for wealth and power -
leaving the service of God for a later hour.
Some people like to have parties and celebrations -
to meet their friends and relations.
Others are content at base - with no fear of losing face,
Some people gaze at the stars - dream of Mercury and Mars.
Others tend a wounded brother love their father and
their mother.
Some people watch the fashion shows -
spending their money as far as it goes.
And others cloose to wear -
just simple ribbons in their hair.

Sr Emily T Hanney

My Blue Lamp

The lamp in the bedroom stands tall
Blue and bright
Not like the others in yellow and white
It still switches on tho' ever so old
Heard lots of stories, new ones and old

It stands up so prominent and watches me sleep
It watches me laugh, get angry and weep
It's not just a lamp it's a friend to me
Nicer than all of the others you see

The one in the kitchen, the one on the stairs
The one on the landing right next to a chair
The one in the bathroom, a clinical white
The one in the lounge a soft creamy light.

The one in the study and one in the hall
The one in the dining room that stands tall
None of these appeal to me
Not like the blue one you see

When I go to bed it's so bright
It allows my parents to peep when I sleep,
But the best thing about it that makes it a heaven
Is that it doesn't go off till half past eleven

Lydia Hall (13)

Time

It's time for this and time for that
It's time to go to bed.
It starts when you're a child
And goes on until you're dead.

Will time erode our lives again
In that somewhere far away
Will we know the difference
Between night and day

Where will we be when time has gone
Over the clouds and far away
Where timeless people live
And day is night and night is day.

Peggy Corr

The Binman's Helper

I'm Sid – the binman's helper
I'm out at early light
For when a Wednesday comes around
I've been up half the night.

They tried to trick me some while back
They changed the binman's day
But it didn't work, I'm well aware
Of the silly games they play.

My job is quite demanding
But I have no need to roam
Because all my working duties
Are very close to home.

I try to help the binmen
By lightening their load
They're always pleased to see me
When they're coming down our road.

I struggle to extract the bones
And smelly bits of fish
I love my job 'most every week
But if I could have one wish

I'd wish each day was Christmas
When I always get the bird
They don't half waste the turkey
It really is absurd.

I use my tiny pointed claws
To make a little tear
I don't know how those men would cope
If I wasn't there.

They pretend that they don't need me
But I know it isn't true
Besides, I like to give a helping hand
Doesn't everyone? Don't you?

I'm a shapely, blue-eyed Siamese
Some people think I'm sweet
But they don't see my shifty look
When I'm searching for some meat.

There's talk of wheelie-bins coming round
I'd hate it if they did
I'm happy with the plastic bags
- I'm the binman's helper - Sid.

Pam S Quigley

Failure

It was on one summer's day in June
that I did change my name.
How could I have ever known that life
would never be the same.

I was, but twenty four that day, my love was pure and true.
My hopes were high, I loved him so,
I never thought my love would go.

I was so very happy then, my heart was full of joy.
Let's have a child, we used to say,
and start off with a little boy.

The years went by with ups and downs,
like everyone must suffer.
A child I did not ever have, how sad,
I never was a mother.

A bungalow for two we brought in a
pretty little market town.
How little did I know one day
my happiness would let me down.

As time went by my love did wane,
he as well, did feel the same.
We grew apart my man and I,
it was a very painful game.

One day could I no longer stand,
the stress, by now, was out of hand,
I had to leave my home behind,
to start a life of another kind.

We got divorced my man and I,
but I no longer sit and cry,
although, at times, I give a sigh,
and then I pause, and wonder why.

L Littlewood

Luck

Some folk, if they fell off a flitting
Would fall in a new pair of shoes
They always seem to be winning things
They never seem to lose.
Now me, well, I'm just the other way
I'm always the first 'Too late'
Even when they're giving out free samples
They always pass my gate.
And I can buy raffle tickets by the dozen
But prizes what get won
Always go to them there folk
Who's only getton one.
Same things happen when sales are on
I can be first in the queue
But I'm the one who gets jammed in
When they open the doors
And all the back enders rush through
By the time I get where I'm going
All the best of the bargains have gone
And the dress I've set my heart on
Somebody else is trying on.
Same when I go on my holiday
I nearly always have to stand in the train
And they could have had weeks of sunshine
When I get there - they've rain
Same thing happens in my love life
I mustn't have what appeals to men
One date with me, and they vanish
And I never see them again
They say you can't be lucky and beautiful
But when you're neither, it's a bit of a mess
So I carry on regardless
And crack on I couldn't care less.

Aye - some folk have all the luck
But on me - I'm sure there's a curse
I'm frightened of wishing my luck would change
'Cos knowing me, it would.
 From bad to worse

A Croston

Christchurch

Boats on the river, all day for me,
Slowly trafficking down to the sea.

Trees by the river spread their sails too,
Copy white canvas - small birds for crew.

I sit here dreaming - trees and boats one,
River and sea-scape haze in the sun.

Elsie Walton

A Holiday

Everybody should have 'A holiday',
Wherever at home or anywhere away,
Weather, it be rain, snow, or in the sun,
Go have fellowship, rest, lots of fun.

Many go abroad, this is their cup of tea,
'A holiday' in the country, or down by the sea,
Some like the red hot sun, so as to get a tan,
Have a nice 'holiday', while you can.
'A holiday', in bonnie Scotland, will do for me,
Places to go, beautiful scenery to see,
Those who can't afford, 'A holiday', save up some money?
Not easy for some, 'A holiday', is sweet as honey.
'Holiday', time is here once more,
Why not go? and you, can explore,
The country, town, seaside, a nice long walk,
Many things to see, meet many different folk,
Enjoy your? 'Holiday', wherever it may be,
Near or far, anywhere, even down by the sea.

Leslie Trotter

Infirmary

An ugly building glow'ring in the mists,
Endless storeys high, faceless concrete slabs.
It seems within its walls no life exists,
That metal chimney skyward thrusts and jabs.
Windows barred and blinds pulled down so tight
Lifeless, faceless, no drama there unfurled.
Mystery, enigma, frustrating sight.
We have no cause to enter this strange world.

Within this hospital lie healing skills;
Nurses, doctors, dedicated, yet drained.
Invasive actions, plethora of pills
Daily dispensed, skilled brains and bodies strained.

A concrete shell with pearls of patient care
Of which some know, but most are unaware.

Elizabeth Hoyle

Good Morning In Our Village Street

'Good morning Mrs so-and-so,
  And how are you today?'
Do I really want to know,
Or is it something just to say?

Oh! dear, here's Mrs Talk-a-lot,
  How shall I get away?
She knows I've had my hair done
  We met yesterday.

Now here comes Mrs Newly-wed.
Looks radiant, as well she might
She caught our local bachelor.
        Almost overnight.

'Well my dear, how nice to see
You young ones back again -'
'You won't be staying! - moving on?'
That's just too bad, the young ones gone.

Ah! Here's the Vicar - gentle, kind,
But something always on his mind.
The Belfrey leaking? Funds to raise?
At times it must be hard to Praise.

Now - Here's my friend, at last I've met
Someone who I want to see
No gossip, just a chat - like me
Being friends to all we meet
In our little village street.

  Gwynneth Carr

65

Gathering Bluebells

Gathering bluebells from bluebell wood
On a carpet of blue and green,
Bells of blue, on long green stems
Sway in the summer hue.
I'll gather an armful
And make a bouquet, with some fern,
For me to take home
To place in a room
And arrange to look good,
These flowers, from bluebell wood.

Marjorie Arnett

Old Girl Sits By Her Fireguard
(This poem was inspired by my late Gran)

Old girl sits by her fire guard,
bloomers drying steam,
off in dreams the old girl flits,
to lands she has never seen.
Old girl sits by her fire guard,
far far away,
thinking of her Lance Corporal,
how they'll be together again. Some day.
Old girl sits by her fire guard,
eyes softly close,
lonely dreams of another widow,
strain on her face now shows.
Old girl sits by her fire guard,
so tired and so worn,
she'll sit in her chair by her fire guard,
till she's found tomorrow morn.
Lonely widow sits by her fire guard,
sleep's her eternal sleep,
together again some forty years on,
her sweetheart she waits to greet.
In Heaven they'll walk hand in hand,
God rejoins them somehow,
to walk God's sundrenched land,
and be together again,
Now . . .

Carl Hales

Friendship

Friendship cannot be bought by anyone,
like love it needs time to grow.
But little acts of kindness and giving
are seeds upon which we can sow.

By helping our neighbours with small things,
by offering that helping hand
a casual acquaintance is deepened
and lets them know that you understand.

True friendship is formed by just caring,
having concern for each others needs.
Putting others feelings first and foremost
and helping so they can succeed.

Just being there for one another.
Being there when upset or low
is a lifeline for those who need us
and is a way our love we can show.

Sheila M Whipp

Two Houses

They both are square,
simple and modern.
Then why I love the one
and not the other?

There's nothing to distinguish
them from so many others,
why then it's only one of them
that all my love so gathers?

House, which was home
in childhood's innocence,
lives in me still, in heart,
in mind, in my subconscience.

All images of beauty
seem to live within its walls
and echo of the happiness
long past, forever calls.

Irena Stankiewicz

A Boomerang

There is a unique missile,
 A boomerang by name,
  Used mainly by Aborigines
  For hunting wild game.

   If you take a boomerang
   And throw it in the air
    It has the knack of coming back
    To the one who threw it there.

     There is a lesson to be learned
     A message to be told,
      of this most unusual tool
       As this analogy will unfold.

      In our daily lives
       Temptation and good abound
        It would seem this innate missile
         In each person can be found.

       How easy it is to fight,
        To quarrel with each other
        How easy to cast the first stone,
        To be victor over another.

     When we are misjudged,
      Nothing is gained by retaliation.
       Silence give such peace to the soul,
       Prayer gives consolation.

    Consider the power of this missile
     Its futility in strife.
    Understand its real significance,
   It can make or mar a life.

So when you use a boomerang,
Don't be harsh - be tender.
Each thought each word, each deed,
May well return - to sender.

Monica Docherty

Buried Alive

How she hit the coffin door,
Begging to be let out.
But when your six foot under,
They can't quite hear your shout.

The thought of maggots crawling in,
Made her stomach begin to convulse.
If only one of a medical profession,
Had thought to check her pulse.

Alan T R Miller

SOS

I want to talk,
but don't know what to say.
I want to shout,
but I feel choked.
I want to cry,
but the tears won't fall.
I want to laugh,
but laughter's far away.
I want to feel,
but I'm confused.
I want to love,
but there's no-one.

I sit in silence
unable to communicate.
Inside I cry . . .
SOS

Ally McCrae

Untitled

My writing can be dreadful, this is a fact I know
I should have been a doctor, Sister tutor told me so
No matter how I practise it never does improve
Except for certain special times when I am in the mood
I'm often quite embarrassed, I'll sign a cheque and then
The sales girl calls the manager, who makes me sign again
Oh how I envy people who write in copper plate
Who sign thing with a flourish and are never made to wait
I had an uncle Jimmy who wasn't all that bright
And even he, at 23 discovered he could write
But then, he had a reason, I believe it's called a schism
He'd nothing else to do all day inside a Nazi prison
But I can never find the time to form a lovely hand
My racing mind expects the pen to match the pace it planned
And so I must apologise to all who strive and strain
To read my rotten writing, I know it is a pain
I bet that all we scrawlers would make a better show
If it hadn't been for just one man, you've guessed it . . . 'Joe Biro'

Patricia Robinson

The Traveller

Every age has its beauty as we travel on through life
In youth we know it all, we take on the 'world and its wife'
We have confidence and strength-we can do anything we please
Fun and happiness is what we seek-our powers will never cease.

Then come the knocks and setbacks-as we travel on past twenty
We're more level headed now, yet still with youth aplenty
On to thirty - a milestone indeed, but still a youthful age
Now with cares: we look back at our youth and feel quite old and
sage.

By forty and fifty we've began to feel the toll of the years
Sixty - we realise we're moving up and begin to have fears
The dreaded threesome and ten mark, we've had the biblical score
'Oh God, I don't want to die-life is good I want some more.'

Where did all those years go, it suddenly seems no time at all -
Who wants to bring back days of youth, we're still having a ball.
Whatever the journey was about, wherever we go from here -
So much joy we had, a glorious life hereafter must be near.

Marjorie K Clarke

My Winter Friend

My little friend the Robin:
He sings in winter's gloom
When other birds are silent
Awaiting summer's noon
Before they flex their voices
And sing some merry tune.

He wears a bright red waistcoat
With suit of velvet brown
And hops along the fences
Of gardens in the town
Until he spies a morsel
Then cheekily swoops down.

So as I dig my garden
He darts around my feet,
Or sits and chirps a greeting
From on the nearby seat.
Then when I turn up an insect
He takes it as a treat.

He brightens up our winter
When all is gloom and cold.
So when I'm wet and weary
My joy is to behold
My little friend the Robin
Who is so bright and bold.

John Whittington

Leaves

Autumn leaves are falling, falling;
Hues of orange, yellow, brown.
Autumn leaves are falling, falling;
Softly, silently, to the ground.

Autumn leaves are swirling higher;
As the wind blows all around.
Autumn leaves are swirling higher;
Listen to the rustling sound.

Autumn leaves are dying, dying;
As the frost begins to bite.
Autumn leaves are dying, dying;
Winter truly is in sight.

But wait . . . new buds will soon appear;
A sign that spring is drawing near.
And leaves, new leaves, in shades of green,
Will dance and sing in the shimmering sheen,
Where the rays of the sun and the dewdrops fall
On those leaves, new leaves, fresh leaves of spring.

Gill Simmons

Si Tu Vas Para Chile
(If You Go To Chile)

You might glimpse her beckoning eyes
Or the flowing fall of her hair
She stands in the doorway and calls
Softly, 'I've been waiting', and dare
You resist those sensuous sighs?
She leads you away to an unknown shrine
Silent you sit, sip your beer, contemplate
Then she comes goddess-like with eyes that shine
Burning, smouldering eyes the colour of slate
Sits close by, speaks her Castillian tongue,
Whispers her words with a willowy song.
'It's time to go'. She guides you gently away
To a rumpled room, but clean and decent
Where you're smothered with love more than a day.

'Ah, no te vayas', said she. Confound her!
It's she who has gone to another town,
But, of course, she'll always remember
That night with you. 'Qué lindo!' She'll moan
And pine, when she's back in the doorway
Sweetly calling:- 'Where have you been,
I was waiting so long?'

Rolf Heming

78

Niagara Falls

Rainbows of many colours
stretching from shore to shore.
Water thundering on both sides
the majesty of water overwhelming.

Green water flowing along
reaching its crescendo, as at its peak -
it topples over with a mighty roar
forming white curtains for all to see.

Inspiring but frightening, the water can be
tho it can be silent, Death's held in its grasp.
Nature reminds, 'Admire but take care
one false step, you're in my lair.'

People gaze in wonderment and awe
so majestic is the waterfall.
Water can be silent as it thunders down
maybe 'Maid of the Mist', she's still around.

Kathy Whitton

Snowdrops

Delicate snow-white petals
Shimmer in frosty air,
Fragile pearls of promise
In bitter landscape bare.

Out of the iron-clad winter,
Ere Blackbird starts to sing,
Green-stemmed, in garden's corner,
The first brave flower of spring.

Bright shafts of sunlight dispelling
The chill mists of January gloom,
Tiny princesses are dancing;
The Snowdrops are in bloom.

Kathy Butler

The Laughing Cactus

My cactus is a funny shape
with spiky points
and graceful curves,
bare quintessential
fat leaves
springing from callused stem.

How does it dare
to fling
such opulent red stars
in all directions?
How has it kept
this secret
for a dingy season,
so it can startle,
thrill us now?

Surely
at its scruffy little heart
is laughter
cascading down the ugly branches,
bursting into song
at the tips!

Elizabeth Wilson

Have You!

Have you heard the birds by the water,
       singing sweetly in tune?
Have you heard the breeze rustle the trees?
       Have you! Have you!

Have you ever seen the wild roses grow,
       tinted pink and single in bloom?
Have you watched a water lily on the lake,
       close up as the sun touched the moon?

Have you seen gnats by the water?
       They hover in the air,
coming closer and closer to you.
       But it's as if they are not there.

Have you seen a dragonfly,
       and the delicateness of its wings?
Its head and tail is a powder blue,
       but it does not have a sting.

There is so much to look at in nature.
       The yellow buttercup in full bloom.
The wild sweet pea, is as violet as can be,
       and the lake has a silver hue.

Wendy Jackson

The Spider's Web

Do we consider the intricate design
Of a spider's web, of gossamer fine?
The beauty is seen after morning dew,
So venture out, when the day is new.
Its shimmering design takes all by surprise
How it's achieved we can only surmise.
We know that later on in the day,
The spider's web will have caught its prey.
When the web is broken or disturbed
The spider works calmly, all unperturbed,
Mending the gaps, his skill supreme
Until at last perfection is seen.
Late summer and autumn is the time
To see this beauty, so sublime.

Many have tried to copy this treasure
With artist's brush, they give full measure,
On stool or seat, midst bracken and bush.
A photo may capture, with colours, that push
All the detail to the fore of the frame
But it's only in three-D we see spider's fame.
From the spider's patience we learn so much.
In renewing our strength, a pause is a must.
We start again, Our Lord is there,
Then humbly offer ourselves in prayer,
For with God's design before our eyes
We can only bow, to the Great and Wise.

Dorothy Parish

A Mother

A mother is there to understand
She is also there to give a hand
A mother's there when you feel sad
She even cares when you are bad

A mother helps you anytime, anywhere
I just call her she's always there
And when you are in deep trouble
She's there for you on the double

A mother picks you up when your down
She even does it without a frown
And when you find you have no friend
She sticks with you till the very end.

Cath Johnston

Abba

You instigated my conception,
And watched me through my birth;
Even before the doctors,
You had seen me first.

Made in the image of God,
I look like my Dad,
You smile on my childish ways
And I make your heart feel glad.

You saw me fall,
When I first walked,
And you listened,
As I started to talk.

You cradled me in your arms,
And protected me in sleep;
You remember my baby days,
And as preciousness, you keep.

You provide for my every breath,
And give me food to eat,
My father, my bread-winner,
You meet all my needs.

I've been so unaware,
So blind and so naive,
Although I hadn't known it,
You were everything to me.

Dee Gallaghue

Familiar

Totally familiar
. . . the memories of love,
care and warmth
flooding and
recalling all those
'safe' memories.

The slight smile
. . . the plump face
. . . those eyes, soft,
forever and forgiving.
A picture of my mother.

Ted Medler

Dear Mum

There is something very peaceful about sitting next to you
Although you sleep and will not wake, there's nothing I can do
To persuade you to drink up your tea or have a bite to eat
But when I sit and hold your hand the peace is such a treat

You teach me to relax and rest - a thing I rarely do
And though you hardly talk at all we communicate with you
Your smile says much, your eyes the rest and gently shake your head
And really in the peace and quiet there's not much to be said.

Your hands are cold, you feel the warmth when my hand covers
                                                    yours
Your eyes flick open, then open wide when Dad walks in the door
He says 'I love you - do you love me?' you say 'I expect I do'
It's just what you'd have said at home, then sleep shuts world from
                                                    view.

I am so glad you're peaceful, I really thank the Lord
It's as if He's very close to you and fills up all the ward
We sing, you tap your fingers, 'Jesus loves me this I know'
And then we hear the strains of other ladies singing low.

They say you are no trouble to the nurses and the staff
They say they love you, talk to you and try to make you laugh
Your hair is brushed, your glasses on, you're spotlessly clean
You always look so comfortable, so peaceful and serene.

We see the Lord's hand in all things - His provision on the night
The empty bed, the staff, the care, His timing is just right
In all the weeks you've been here and every time we call
We know the Lord is with us and with you - He loves us all.

Olive Blackwell

87

To Claire (an unseen new arrival)

Welcome, welcome little Claire
Though you be ginger, dark or fair
With tiny toes and laughing eyes
Or bravely bald with tubby thighs!

Welcome to Computerland
Where floppy discs are close at hand
And chips are fed into machines -
No longer eaten with baked beans.

Perhaps some day you'll be a Guide
And wear your Trefoil Badge with pride
And camp in weather fair or damp
Without a sunshade or a gamp.

And welcome, welcome Claire Louise,
To summer skies and bumblebees,
To gurgling streams and mountains high
And skylarks soaring in the sky.

And welcome, welcome little dove,
To caring, sharing, giving, love
And may life bring you joy and peace
And pleasure that may never cease.

Eileen M Pratt

Spare The Rod And Spoil The Child
A true story

Old John and Mary were parents
Who both loved their little son Chris.
A child of remarkable talents,
Rich jewel in their late wedded bliss.

Young Chris was always the schemer,
With taunts ever urging his pals
To join him in all his rash ventures,
Escapades both dangerous and bad.

His parents now bent and aged,
Chris soon made friends beyond home.
They led him to unlawful ventures,
Oft stealing and plundering the stores.

One night a misfortune hit Chris
As he signalled to warn his pals
Police pounced instantly upon him,
While his friends got away with the spoils.

Then they questioned and queried and
Promised him freedom, if only
All the names of his pals he would tell
But Chris remained silent and surly.

At last before the Judge Chris stood
'Young man you are here accused of
Aiding and abetting some felons,
Are you guilty or are you not?' 'No'.

'No what?' 'No Sir'. 'No Sir what?' 'Well,
You honour I am not guilty'.
'Since you refuse to name the culprits
Sentence on you must be passed - Guilty!'

Straight back to his cell they led him,
Deportation for life they said!
He thought of his frail old Mother and
Instead of a blessing he cursed her.

Just ere the ship had raised anchor
Chris in a loud voice petitioned -
Let me whisper a word in Ma's ear
To remind her she once had a son.

With arms outstretched she met him with
Tears running down her pale cheeks;
A convict I am 'cause you spoilt me'
He said and bending bit off her ear.

Elizabeth O'Mahony

A Mother's Love

If our Mums didn't love us or show they care,
Then we ourselves would have nothing to share,
For a Mother's love is passed on and on,
A Mother's love is never done.

It keeps on loving through thick and thin,
And covers over multitudes of sin,
She makes us feel we're the very best,
We can face the storm, pass every test.

So as you live your life each day,
Show her in all you do and say,
That you love her and are thankful too,
For all the love she's shown to you.

Kerry Ann Watson

Nan's Day

We really need a Nan's day,
For the best nan in the world,
And they can go play bingo,
And get their hair curled.

We really need a Nan's day,
To keep all the nans happy,
When they open up their presents,
No longer needing a nanny.

I really need a Nan's day,
To show my love for nan,
I'll give her a great big pressie
Because she is supergran!

Anne Marie Hackett

Mother's Day

M-other's Day once a year, only in May, some say.
O-n the reverse I say it takes place every day!
T-oday or tomorrow, in ups and downs, alone,
H-ello Mummy, you hear over there when I phone?
E-ven when far away will you keep harm from me
R-ight from the sunny realm of your Eternity?
'
S-hed your light on the dark days and ways of despair,

D-addy used to tell us: 'To her you should be fair.'
A-nd life taught us we aren't able to buy such a jewel,
Y-es, you bore us, shaped us, died . . . Thanks, you are noble.

P Jean

My Grand-Daughters

As a grandmother I'm so very proud
To have lovely grand-daughter's around,
I miss you all so much each day
But you know that I'll still love you
        come what may.
You are to me a sense of pride
            and joy
Nothing anyone in this world can destroy
This little poem comes with love and kisses
Because you're all someone that your
        Nan badly misses.

D Gooch

Christ's Sacrifice

Thank you Lord, thank you Lord, For your wondrous mercy.

Thank you Lord for all your love
Thank you for your giving,
Thank you for the life you gave,
All our sins forgiving,
All our sins forgiving.

Please forgive our lack of love,
Please forgive our coldness
Help us Lord, to live our lives
Showing forth your boldness
Showing forth your boldness

Praise the Lord that we can share,
Share what He has given,
Let us now give praise to Him,
For our sins forgiven
For our sins forgiven

Jesus gave His life for all,
Gave in love so tender,
Let us give our lives to Him,
All to Him surrender,
All to Him surrender.

Anne Gray

Love

Love, sweet mystery of life;
Whence comes its fragrance?
Wondrous adornment of creations crown
Bestowed by Him who doeth all things well.

The colours of the rainbow are not seen
Except the sunshine's rays make clear their view!
Then what of us who from the light turn back
And hide from Him who would make all things new?

Within our hungry hearts are yearnings unfulfilled
That speak of emptiness. How then can
We find joy who truth refuse to own
And yet pretend to know the One who love us so?

M Reader

Glorious Easter Day

I can't believe they've crucified my Jesus.
I can't believe that he is really dead.
They mocked and scorned, and tortured him most cruelly,
And put a crown of thorns upon his head

They cast lots for the robe from off his body.
They did not care that he should suffer so.
He said 'Forgive them, they know not what they're doing,'
Just before it was time for him to go.

He died in such lonely isolation.
From him 'most all his friends around did flee.
Such despair he felt, that he himself had called out,
'My God, why hast thou forsaken me?'

And yet, he gave back to God his spirit
Ere his last breath he finally did draw.
He died for us his heavenly home to inherit
If we pass on his good news for evermore.

Because upon that famous Easter morning
The tomb was empty, and the stone rolled right away.
Each one of us now has a grand new dawning.
The Lord has risen on glorious Easter day.

Margaret M Sherwood

Fullness Of Life

I have come that they may
have life, and have it to the
full (John 10;10 NIV)

Jesus, you promised life in its fullness,
Life more abundant, for which I pray;
Blessings unceasing, joy without measure,
Grace all sufficient, strength for each day;
Help in my weakness, peace through your calming,
Comfort in sorrow through love's embrace;
And in your service fruitful achievement:
Life in its fullness! Gift of your grace!

Life in its fullness! Life in its richness!
Your life, O Mater, lived out in me;
This is my longing! This is my claiming!
Life in its fullness! Your gift to me.

What then could hinder my own attaining
Life in its fullness offered to me?
Show me, my Master, through your revealing,
Tenderly guiding, help me to see:
Then give me courage, knowing my weakness,
Humbly, yet trusting, failures to face,
Seeking your mercy, cleansing and healing,
Finding renewing through your rich grace.

Life in its fullness! Glad my rejoicing!
Proving the marvels your love bestows,
Knowing your blessings, goodness and mercy,
Wondrous attainment, joy overflows:
Daily refreshing through my communing,
As when the branches stay in the vine,
Sweetens my service, thrills my devotion:
Life in its fullness! Your life is mine!

David Barker

Prelude To Easter

Precious is this season which follows winter's hidden industry -
Revival bursting out of slumbering earth, still half-frozen.
Insects astir, brilliant daubs of colour - bumble bees and ants by the
dozen
Never ceasing activity around the buds of the pussy willow tree.
Tentative green banners arise, piercing through virgin ground so
recently
Enveloped in the soft white radiance of protecting snow.
Messengers of God's fabulous creation, teeming new life on the go -
Praise to him the artist of the sun-kissed flowers, a myriad of
pastel hues and golden glory -
Springs refreshing stir in the air, bird song heralds the
triumphant risen dawn of
Jesus Glorified,
Easter's story.

Mary Bréchemier

Carpenter's Cross
(After A E Housman)

Once in the day when heaven descended
And earth's pretensions threadbare fled
A Carpenter, his calling ended,
Served for his wages and was dead.

His work was of so high a value
That no man found could match its worth -
So perfect that it was I tell you
Too fine a thing for this poor earth.

For when with infinite resources
Of grace and skill he plied his trade,
The hands of envy rallied forces -
The Carpenter a cross they made

Whereon twixt earth and sky suspended
His hands held back all heaven above;
What God indicted He defended,
And saved the Universe for Love.

Edward Smyth

The Lamb

Driving around the countryside
One bright December morn.
I noticed in the fields of sheep
Some baby lambs were born.
>Now we remember
>The birth of Jesus in December.
Lambs at Christmas time, born to live
And play and eat, then die.
Destined for someone's Sunday lunch,
With mint sauce standing by.
>See the lamb who came
>To die for us on a cross of shame.
When the Israelites left Egypt.
The Passover took place.
A male lamb was killed and eaten
With herbs, in every case.
>God said he would give
>A Passover lamb, so that we could live.
'This is my body given for you,
Eat and remember me'.
Whoever eats this bread of life
Will live in Jesus-free.
>'Take this cup of wine,
>It's a promise sealed with blood of mine'.
Worthy is the lamb who was slain,
To receive strength and praise.
Wisdom and honour and glory
Unto Jesus we raise.
>With angels in heaven
>We will sing for evermore, amen!

Pat Tilsley Green

Where Have They Gone?

Where have they gone they that said
they would die for me?
Have they fled hurrying away
exclaiming they never knew me?

But they will know this hour of betrayal,
it will lay heavy on their hearts.
O! the sadness of this day
death enjoy thy triumph.
Of torture and humiliation,
for thy allotted reign is short,
but three days.

O! frightened souls see the dark tomb
opened, radiant with my love.
Bursting, spreading, overpowering
doubts and despair.
This is the resurrection!
Where have they gone?
but they will return
to see the empty tomb.

Mavis Catlow

Easter Song

Let all the world rejoice and sing upon this Easter Day
Jesus Christ is risen, the stone has rolled away.
On the cross He suffered pain so hard to bear, but
His Loving Father heard His fervent prayer.

Earth could not contain Him, thought He was born as man
God's own Son, our Saviour, was the Father's plan.
Born of a Virgin, Mary, a manger for a King,
Love and endless mercy His the gift to bring.

For the love of sinners He died that we might live
Raised up by His Father, we must trust, believe,
As we seek to serve Him, for the truth sets free
Reborn to humbly follow, we too the Lord shall see.

Sing the song of Easter beneath His cross to find
Peace and sweet redemption bought for humankind
Seeking His forgiveness from every sin and shame,
Blessings ever flowing from His Holy name.

Joan Heybourn

Easter Morning Glory

As sudden sunshine broke the night
And chased the stars away,
To usher in the day;
So songs of joy mixed with the light,
Pure music from a radiant height,
As sudden sunshine broke the night
And chased the stars away.

Now butterflies stretch out their wings
And bid farewell to night,
With consummate delight;
A blackbird in the garden sings
Of glad inconsequential things,
As butterflies stretch out their wings
And bid farewell to night.

The flowers in the garden raise
A hymn of utter joy,
No storm clouds could destroy;
They offer to their Maker praise,
And nature lovers see His ways,
As flowers in the garden raise
A hymn of utter joy.

Caroline Birchmore

The Garden Tomb

The quietness of a garden tomb,
A body swathed in cloth,
Surrounded by the broken hopes
Of those who loved the Lord.
The High Priests sealed the rock hewn tomb
And posted guards to watch.
They meant to see the Way was dead,
And Christ no more be seen.
During the quietness of the night
An earthquake shook the land,
And angels came to move the stone,
God's miracle to show.
The soldiers fell, as though in death,
For fear had filled their hearts,
And later went to tell the Priests,
Who bought their silence dear.
As dawn drew near the women came,
With herbs to treat the corpse.
They found the stone was rolled away
And angels waited there,
To tell the world that Christ still lives,
And gives the world new hope.
The women took this message new
And told the men, 'He lives'
From that lonely garden tomb
New hope the world received,
That we with Him can live again,
Through faith in God's own Son.

Sheila E Groom

106

The Black Fast

Holding fast to the thorn,
Pain through his body torn,
Not for him was light by light
The grey goose had left the bay.
Slowly creamed out of the water
Came the fairest calling high,
Taller and taller still,
Came that God from on high.
He stepped down from yonder thorn.
Me he saw, broken beaten upon the shore.
Taking high my hand of begging.
Filled with delights and a creed.
He the author, high and fast,
Black fast - no food to feed,
Black fast freedom food.
Honour him who is the King,
Who wore around his head the thorn
To break the fast.
Black fast.

Sylvia Chambers

The Eucharist

'This is my body;' the words ring out;
Christ is present, there is no doubt
That once again, as in days of old
Something more precious than silver and gold
Is here for us, that we may feed
And satisfy our deepest need
For God, who gave His Son that we
Might join with Him in unity,
As on that consecrated bread
Our hungry souls are truly fed.
'This is my Blood;' the wine is changed
So once again, as He arranged
His people can receive a drink
Surpassing all that they could think
That God might give them; but His love
Flowed to earth from heaven above
And through His Son gave man a gift
To heal the damage of the rift
That had been caused when Adam's sin
Broke the bond and entered in
Between mankind and God on high;
Christ's death meant man no more need die.
He rose; and now through bread and wine
His faithful people on Him dine.

Eileen Morrison

Easter Time

Lambs may prance around the fields
And children laugh with glee
What about God's precious son
Who died for you and me.

I would just like to tell you
What Easter means to me
It's the time I celebrate Christ's death
And glorious victory.

He came into this life to be
The sacrificial lamb
To shed his blood upon a tree
For the souls of sinful man.

What does Easter mean
To those who know not Christ
Who never heard he made
For them the sacrifice.

Upon a cruel cross he hung
He took your place and mine
So think about what he has done
Remember Easter Time

B M Smyth

Masks

You don't want to know the real me,
The one you can see is a mask,
I don't really want to be free,
I don't feel I'm up to the task.
You see me as peaceful and calm -
Inside I'm as wild as the sea.
I don't want to cause you alarm,
You don't want to know the real me.

You wouldn't want me as a friend,
It's not that I'm spiteful at heart,
I'm afraid I would fail in the end,
I'm just used to playing a part.
You see what I want you to see,
I feel that I have to pretend
There's nothing the matter with me -
You wouldn't want me as a friend.

Please help me to find the real me,
I'm tired of living a lie,
I know that I need to be free,
Perhaps with your help I could try.
The mask is so hard to let go,
And easier, maybe, to see,
But it will be worth it, I know -
Please help me to find the real me.

Catherine French

Success

I've got to make it!
I'm gonna make it!

What do I have to do?
Where do I have to go?

Have faith is the first answer,
To the end is the second.
Okay . . . so far, so good.

How far must I go . . .?
. . . All the way.

When will I know I've reached?
. . . When you've found relief!

I've made it . . . !
I've succeeded . . . !
And yes you can too . . . !

Dionne McLean

God Knows

I sometimes wonder
If I've made a difference
To anyone's life
Save being a wife
And mother.
Not that that's not important
Its been my mainstay
Not having 'my way'
But bending to others
If you see what I mean.
I love them so dearly
But clearly
There is another dimension
To life.
So
What is the difference
That I may have made?
God knows.
I'll find out one day
When it's too late to say
What deeds have been done
Or lack of them.
He'll tell me.

Audrey Hardy

Wonders

My Mammy my Daddy I called them
No need for 'my' the teacher said.
Loving God, each other, us, our land,
My Mammy would recite poetry
Tell us stories of long-ago
Radio dramas, self-composed sagas
Bake cakes from yeast plump whiteness
Make blackberry jam, marmalade, crab apple jelly
Doughnuts, pies, sweet treats galore
Rich stews, meat cakes, dumplings
In winter dancing 'Nuts in May'
She warmed us for a lifetime.
Friendly stars majestic moon lighted the path
To our door

My Daddy quiet, quick-tempered, strict, humorous
Often joking, seaming our childhood with laughter
Polishing our shoes, bathing us, gently drying our hair
He supplied darts, ring-board, chess, bingo
Tops for the whipping season, bow arrow
Money for travelling theatre
Sunday train trips to the summer sea
He would fly his American box-kite, reminding
St Peter and us, that we were on the way
Whispering, he would light-lift a branch
Show us a nesting bird with gawping fledglings
We would listen at my Daddy's promptings
To the corncrake beyond the old wooden gate
He taught us to swim and float toe to toe
Borne on the calm river to stately seas of awesome sky

Close to the rockfield my Mammy would spread
The cloth in the dining room, a hedged green space with adjoining
parlour
Well-fed, exercised, exalted, we mused
As she lilted simple prayers
Heaven's windows twinkling in her telling of joy, sorrow, glory

These events were a long time ago
My Mammy my Daddy are where she said: 'Don't fret'
'I'll be able to do alot more for you when I'm gone'-
My family can sure expect wonders

Bella Carroll

Truth

The lake of fear,
Feeding on guilt,
Just one escape
Through fire to the truth.

Innocence fades,
Constructing our sin,
Digging a hole,
No escape, fall in.

There is only one light
Which can overturn hell,
Revelation ignites
The truth you can't tell.

The world is alive
With fear and heartache,
But nobody sees
That we're all just a fake.

What a burden for all,
With no hope to sustain,
It seems by pure chance
We are born again.

Kneel before me
And submit your will,
Look at the truth,
Else consumed, kill.

G Bevan

Monday

Woke up this morning it's Monday again,
Looked out of the window it's pouring with rain,
Baby's crying I've got to go,
Glad that you're there God.

Off to the shops baby in tow,
Why is the traffic moving so slow?
Look at that bird how can he sing?
It's because you're here God.

Lunchtime soon I'll have a rest.
Let's go to a café that one looks best,
I'll have a sandwich baby a cake,
Rest awhile with us God.

Home now baby there's chores to do,
Sweeping, cleaning and some ironing too,
Sleep now baby just awhile,
This is my time with God.

Teatime now the family's due,
Hope it's nice this recipe's new,
Come on baby you sit there,
Please come dine with us God.

Bedtime now the day is through,
Rest now baby the angels are due,
Hear their voices their greetings ring,
Thank you God for everything.

Pauline Chambers

Street Life

A little old lady walks the streets,
Head hung low, no shoes on her feet.
Dirt on her clothes and dirt in her hair,
'Why is life so unfair.'

She begs for money and begs for food,
But, the response is cruel and always rude.
Without a friend and a loving home,
She wanders the roads all alone.

At night you can hear her softly weeping,
While everyone else is warm and sleeping.
Dreaming of the life she once had,
Before it went so terribly bad.

I know this lady and you do too,
She's the one, who seeks help from you.
When she sits on the corner of the street,
And begs for money and food to eat.

So, next time you see her don't walk by,
With a stare, a tut, and a sigh.
Give her a smile, and help her too,
'Cos you never know it could have been you!

K Tooth

Life

Life is very wonderful
Of that there is no doubt
And absolutely delightful,
If one can go out and about.

Each moment is sublime
And certainly worthwhile.
If you do but take time,
To give a little smile.

Now always enjoy each day
And give thanks to God above,
Who will guide you on your way,
To His home of eternal love.

Helen Allan

Life Is What You Make It

Life is what you make it
It can be good or bad
Depending on the choices you make
Which will make you happy or sad
We don't always have a choice
About what comes our way.
Circumstances differ each and every day
No matter who or what we are
No one is free from ill
You worry fret and struggle
Can't seem to be calm and still
God doesn't want us to struggle and strive
Our burdens we can unload
And travel safely with him
Along the narrow road
Jesus didn't say we'd be trouble free
But I know for sure he is there with me
Sharing my joy, my heartache and pain
Giving comfort and peace, again and again
Though life is what you make it
Don't go it on your own
Put your trust in Jesus
And you'll never feel alone.

W Barrett

Have A Nice Day

Write me a poem, what shall I write?
About the weather, or time of day,
Is the sun shining, clear and bright?
Well that is not so, I need to say.

I look through my window, and what do I see?
People with motorcars, on their way.
I wonder in half an hour, where will they be?
From where I am looking I cannot say

None of my business yes that is true,
I hope they all make it, with no regret.
All with so many things to do,
Some may not be at their place of work yet.

I wish them all safety with lots of care,
So when they arrive, can shout 'Hooray'.
But there's much more to follow, so let's be fair,
Give them a cheer shouting 'Have a nice day'

With all their worries, and cares of the day,
Doing their job, as best they can.
Spare just a moment, to look up and say.
Thank God, I made it, 'Just once again'.

Ernest Stephen Swan